Who was Hercules?

Greek Mythology for Kids
Children's Greek &
Roman Books

BABY PROFESSOR

EDUCATION KIDS

Speedy Publishing LLC

40 E. Main St. #1156

Newark, DE 19711

www.speedypublishing.com

Copyright 2017

To the ancient Greeks, gods made storms and earthquakes, and heroes fought monsters just over there, beyond the next hill.

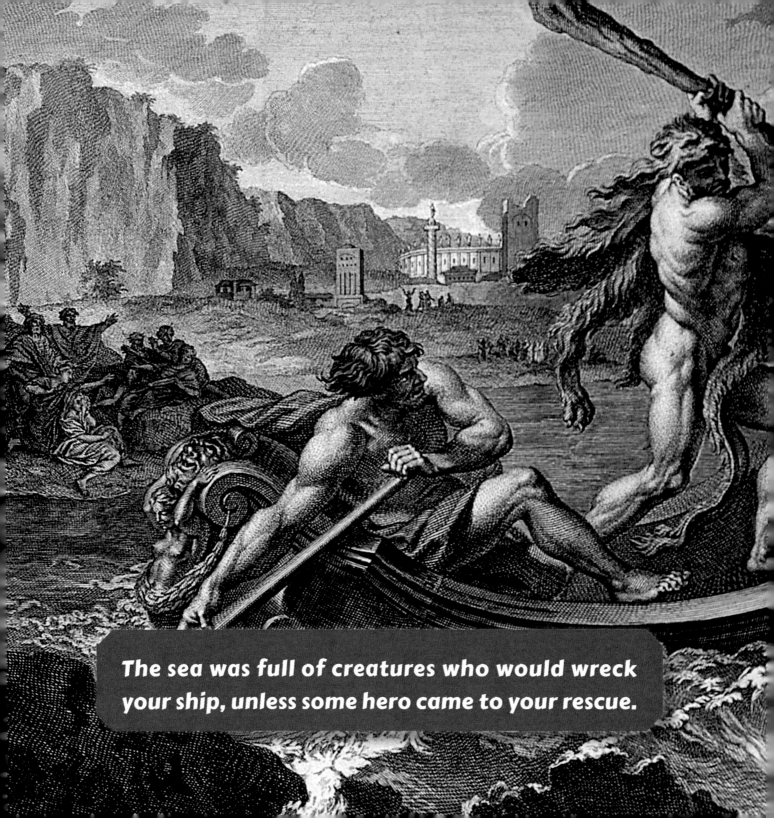

The sea was full of creatures who would wreck your ship, unless some hero came to your rescue.

One of the greatest heroes was Hercules. Let's find out about him.

Who was Hercules?

Zeus, king of the gods, fell in love with Alcmene, a human. Zeus took the form of Alcmene's husband and slept with her to make her pregnant. Hercules was therefore a demi-god: half-human and half-god.

Hercules was very strong from his birth. And it was a good thing he was! Hera, the wife of Zeus, was angry at Zeus for having a baby with a mortal woman. Hera sent two large snakes to kill the baby Hercules, but Hercules, even before he could walk or talk, was able to kill both the snakes.

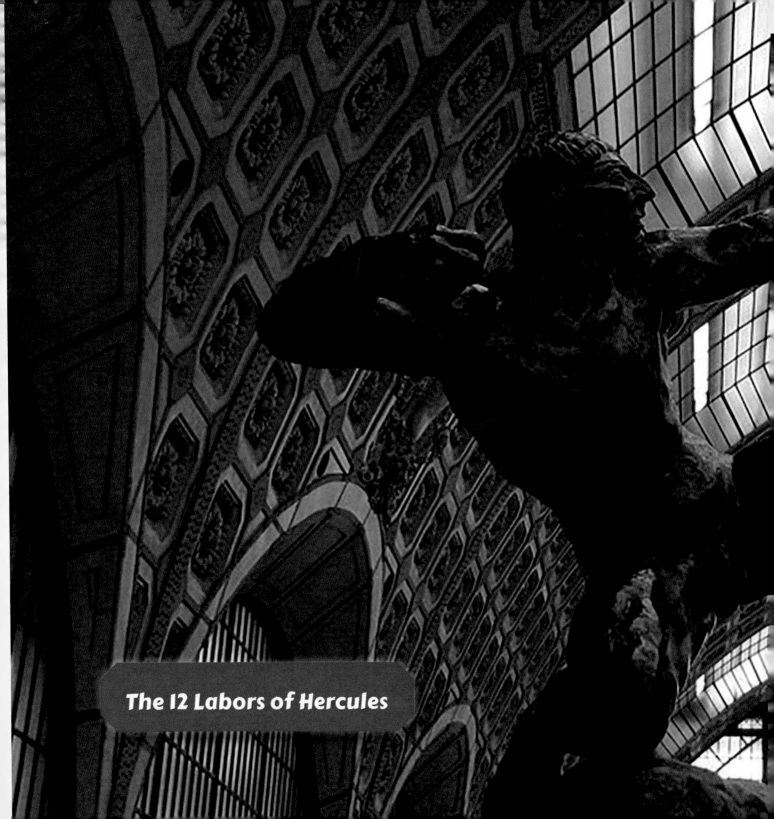

The 12 Labors of Hercules

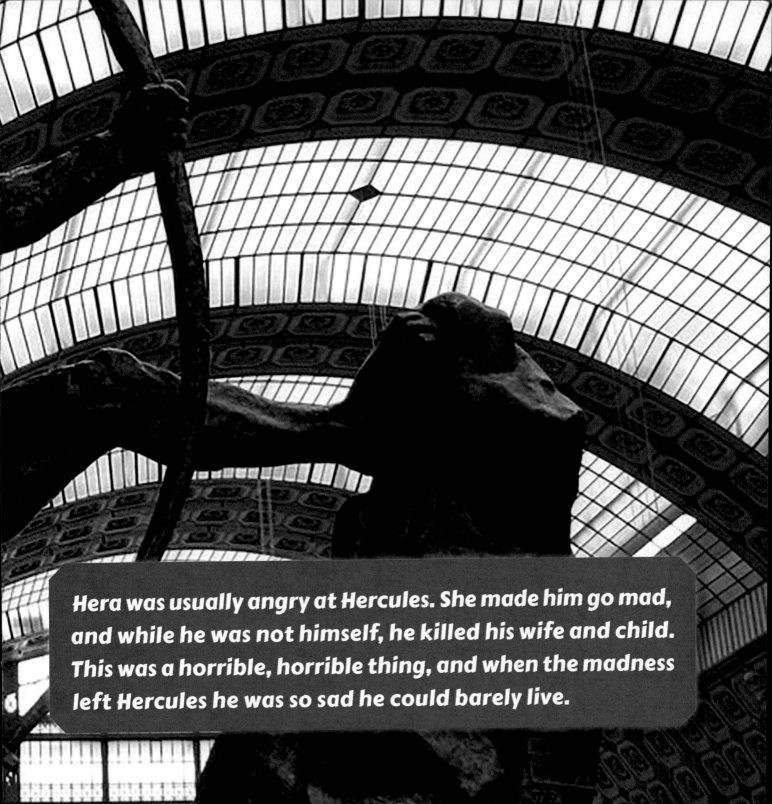

Hera was usually angry at Hercules. She made him go mad, and while he was not himself, he killed his wife and child. This was a horrible, horrible thing, and when the madness left Hercules he was so sad he could barely live.

Finally Hercules went to the Oracle at Delphi to find out what he should do to atone for his horrible deed.

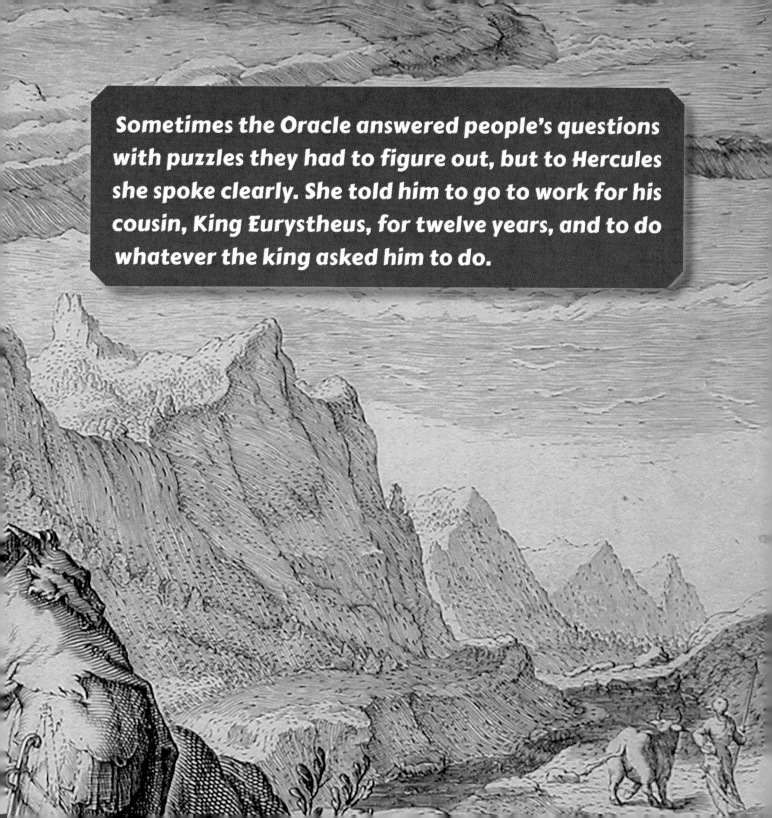

Sometimes the Oracle answered people's questions with puzzles they had to figure out, but to Hercules she spoke clearly. She told him to go to work for his cousin, King Eurystheus, for twelve years, and to do whatever the king asked him to do.

So Hercules went to the king to work off his sorrow and guilt. The king set him job after job, and Hercules did each one.

Here are the twelve jobs, or "labors", Hercules performed for King Eurystheus:

Kill the Lion of Nemea

The Nemean Lion was said to capture women and hold them hostage in a cave. When heroes tried to rescue the women, the lion would attack and eat them.

Hercules tried to shoot the lion with arrows, but its fur and hide were like armor.

Hercules finally knocked the lion down with his club (a favorite weapon) and then choked the lion to death.

Defeat the Lernaean Hydra

The Hydra was a nine-headed monster that Hera had created to destroy Hercules. Its lair was filled with poisonous fumes, so Hercules had to wear a mask over his face.

He found that every time he cut off one of the Hydra's heads, two heads grew back. Finally Hercules' nephew, Lolaus, came up with the idea of burning the stump after each head was cut off, to stop new heads from growing.

In the end, Hercules managed to cut off the Hydra's one immortal head. Hera put the Hydra in the night sky as a constellation.

Capture the Ceryneian Hind

King Eurystheus set Hercules a task that did not involve killing. He had to catch the Ceryneian Hind, a large animal like a deer that had antlers of gold and hooves of brass. The animal was so fast that it could run faster than an arrow could fly.

The animal was sacred to the goddess Artemis, and the king and Hera hoped that, if Hercules succeeded, Artemis would become angry with him and destroy him.

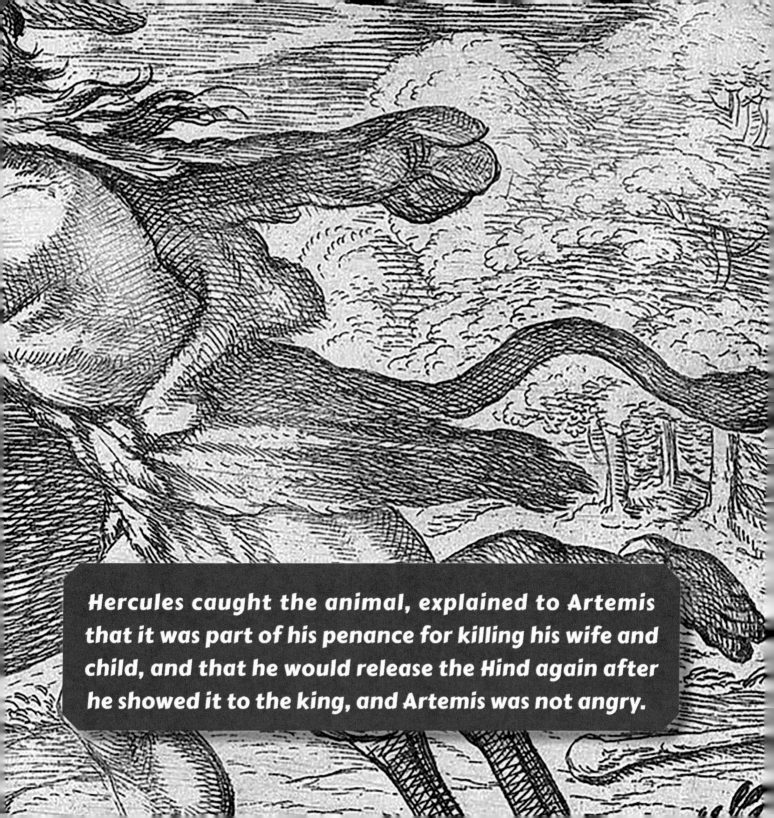

Hercules caught the animal, explained to Artemis that it was part of his penance for killing his wife and child, and that he would release the Hind again after he showed it to the king, and Artemis was not angry.

Capture the Erymanthian Boar

For his next labor, Hercules had to capture a powerful giant boar, or male pig, and bring it back to the king. Hercules had to track the animal all over Greece for a year and could not figure out how to catch it without killing it.

The centaur Chiron told Hercules to drive the animal into thick snow, where it could not move quickly or fight well. Hercules did this and brought the Boar to the king, who was so frightened of it that he hid in a big metal pot that was half-buried in the ground until Hercules took the Boar away again.

Clean the Augean Stables in just one day

King Eurystheus thought Hercules would refuse the next labor and so fail. Hercules had to clean the stables belonging to King Augeas.

Nobody had cleaned the stables in 30 years, and the 1000 immortal beasts who lived there produced tons and tons of dung.

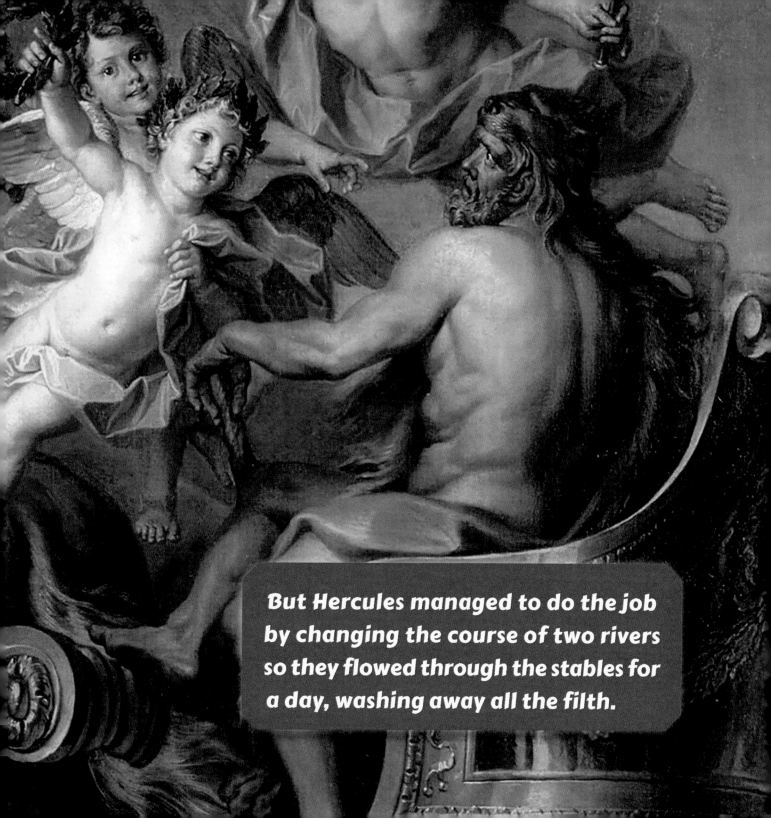

But Hercules managed to do the job by changing the course of two rivers so they flowed through the stables for a day, washing away all the filth.

Kill the Birds of Stymphalia

The birds ate people, and had bronze beaks and sharp feathers they could send like arrows at their enemies. They had poisoned the land around Lake Stymphalia. Hercules got a special rattle from the goddess Athena. He shook the rattle to scare the birds into the air, and then shot many of them with his bow and arrows. The rest flew away.

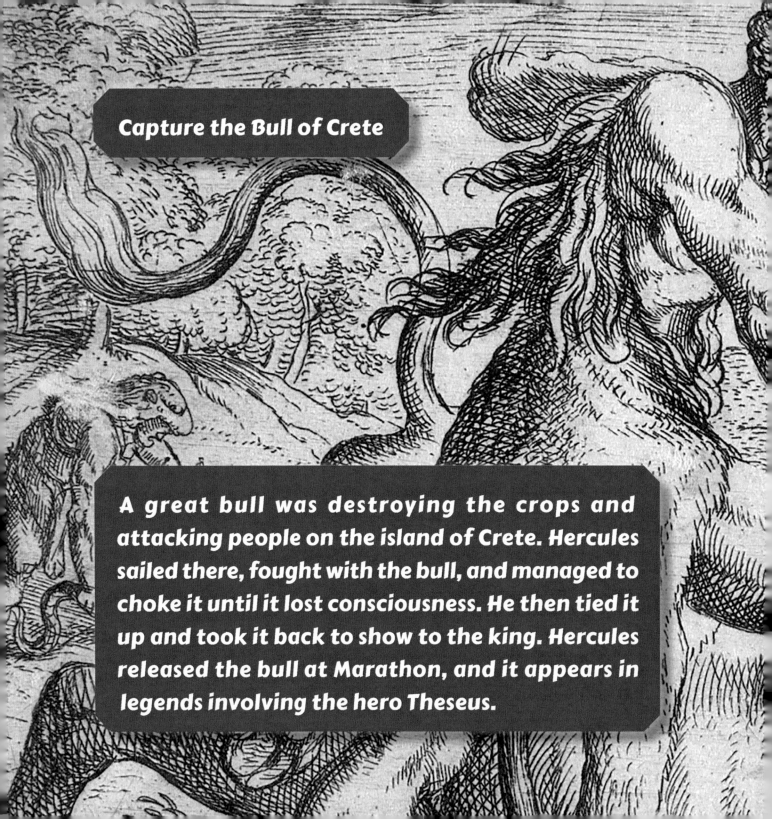

Capture the Bull of Crete

A great bull was destroying the crops and attacking people on the island of Crete. Hercules sailed there, fought with the bull, and managed to choke it until it lost consciousness. He then tied it up and took it back to show to the king. Hercules released the bull at Marathon, and it appears in legends involving the hero Theseus.

Steal the Horses of Diomedes

King Diomedes had four powerful horses who were wild and dangerous. Diomedes fed them human flesh, which made them crazy.

Hercules defeated and killed king Diomedes, and fed him to the horses, which somehow made them calmer. He then could take them to King Eurystheus.

Take a belt from Hippolyta, Queen of the Amazons

King Eurystheus' daughter wanted a special present, so Hercules travelled to take a special belt from the Amazon Queen, Hippolyta.

Hera got involved in the story, making the Amazons hate and distrust Hercules. In the end, Hercules had the belt, but Queen Hippolyta, who had wanted to give it to him, was dead.

Steal cattle from Geryon, a monster

This labor had so many stages, and so many adventures, that it would make a book all by itself! Hercules had to travel far to the west to get the cattle, and then had to bring them back to King Eurystheus despite monsters and buzzing flies that Hera sent to make the cattle run away.

Bring back the apples of the Hesperides

To the Greeks, the Hesperides were islands far to the west where the titan Atlas stood, holding up the sky. Hercules had to take Atlas' place while the titan collected the apples, and then trick Atlas into taking the sky onto his shoulders again.

Capture and bring back Cerberus

Cerberus was the three-headed dog who guarded the underworld for its lord, the god Hades. To even approach the underworld, Hercules had to learn mystic rituals. While in the underworld he encountered shades of the dead and living heroes, like Theseus, who were being held captive.

Hercules freed Theseus, and then asked Hades if he could take Cerberus to show to King Eurystheus. Hades agreed, if Hercules could capture Cerberus without hurting the dog. Hercules succeeded, showed the dog to the king, and then took the dog back to the underworld.

My favorite part of this labor is the name of this powerful, scary, three-headed creature. Cerberus is from the Greek word for "spotted". So the fearsome god of the underworld, Hades, named its terrible guardian and his pet, "Spot"!

Hercules appears in many more stories and adventures, sometimes saving people from monsters and sometimes dodging Hera, who went on hating him. His favorite weapons were a club, and a bow with poisoned arrows.

The death of Hercules

Hercules died because of a trick played on him. With his wife Deianeira nearby, Hercules was fighting a centaur (a creature who is half-person, half horse). Hercules shot the centaur with an arrow that had poison on its tip.

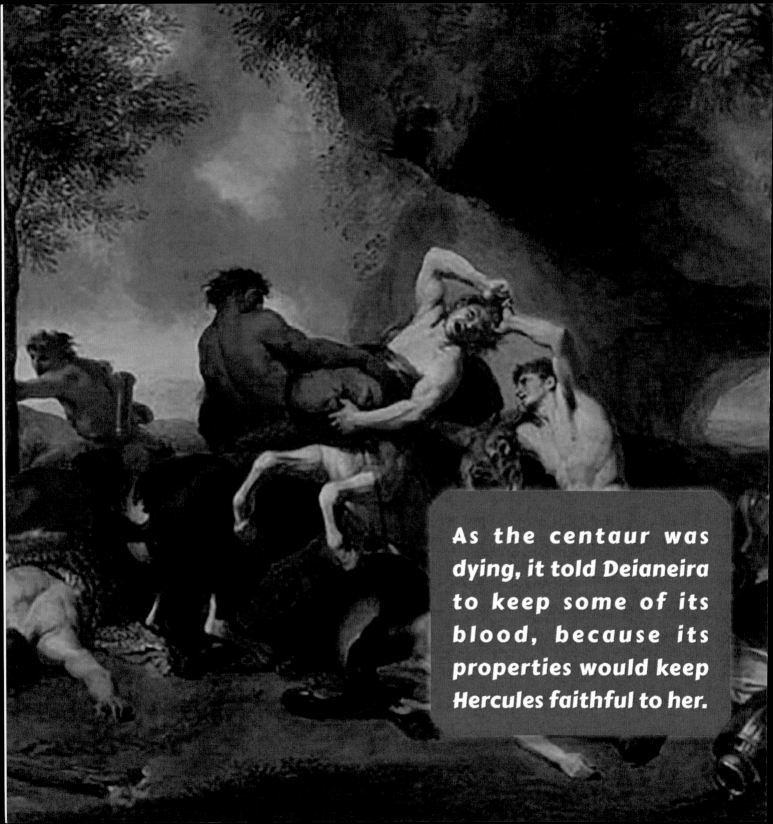

As the centaur was dying, it told Deianeira to keep some of its blood, because its properties would keep Hercules faithful to her.

Deianeira believed the centaur. Later, when she thought Hercules was getting interested in another woman, she soaked his shirt in the blood, thinking this would keep Hercules in love with her.

But the blood was a poison. When Hercules wore the shirt, the poison soaked into him and started to burn him up. There are many versions of what happened next, but the result is the same: Hercules died a painful death. Because he was a demi-god, after his death on earth Hercules went to live with the gods on Mount Olympus.

Hercules fought so many monsters, you would think he would have solved all of Greece's problems! But the Greeks had a lot of monsters and enemies in its stories and myths, and needed many heroes and many friendly gods to help them. Other Baby Professor books, like Apollo's Deadly Bow and Arrow, can help you learn about more exciting Greek myths and heroes.